Simply Afghan

Afghan recipes for the American home cook

Kochai Farhad

Authored with Joseph Mansoor Saleh

Copyright © 2014 Kochai Farhad & Joseph Mansoor Saleh

All rights reserved.

ISBN-13:
978-1500812126

ISBN-10:
1500812129

DEDICATION

For my mother and keeping her recipes alive. *1975 in Kabul*

A portion of proceeds will go towards teaching the women of Afghanistan employment skills.

CONTENTS

	Introduction	i
1	Soups	1
2	Rice	13
3	Stews	25
4	Kabobs	35
	About Author	45

INTRODUCTION

I didn't begin cooking until I was in my late thirties. This is a huge offense in the Afghan culture for women. Young girls in their early teens usually know how to cook a full dinner in order to even be considered a proper Afghan woman. I was raised in a huge family, and this was probably a handicap for me since there was no need for me to cook. In my defense, I possessed other household skills like sewing that I relied upon.

Once I immigrated to America with my family and was ready for marriage, I realized that cooking was an important skill to learn. Fast forward to newlywed life and pregnancy: my partner at the time only knew how to cook white rice (*Chalow*) and a really awful chicken dish (*Qorma*). After a few days of this, I turned to my mother and slowly began to learn how to cook Afghan recipes.

Almost thirty years later, I am constantly entertaining friends and family, receiving endless compliments on my cuisine. For that reason, I would like to give American home cooks the hope and opportunity to learn an exciting and exotic cuisine in the comfort of their own home.

1   SOUPS - SHORWA

Often made in Afghanistan as a way to extend produce, especially meats, soups *(shorwa)* make a great meal. Comforting and soothing, prepare these *shorwas* with love for you and your family.

I remember when...

I was seven years old and it was really cold in Kabul. I had gotten the flu and my mother made me some *Shorwa Berenj*. I didn't want to eat anything, but with the insistence of my mother, I had some. Even in that sick state, I could not stop eating. She was right, I felt so much better the next day and alas, had to go to school.

Shorwa Berenj recipe on page 6

Lamb & Potato Soup ❖ *Shorwa-e-Gosphand*

<u>1 hour 15 minutes cooking time</u> (serves 4)
<u>Ingredients:</u>
2 medium yellow onions peeled and chopped
2 lb. lamb shank cut into 2-inch cubes
2 russet potatoes peeled and cut into 1 inch cubes
3 roma tomatoes rough chopped
1 can garbanzo beans 15oz. drained
3 cloves garlic minced
¼ cup fresh cilantro chopped
6 cups boiling hot water
4 tablespoons canola oil
1 teaspoon turmeric
2 teaspoons salt & black pepper to taste

In a large pot, sauté onions in canola oil until translucent. Rinse and add lamb. Add turmeric and garlic. Sauté lamb until brown. Add tomatoes and cook until incorporated. Add boiling hot water and cover pot, simmer on medium low heat for 45 minutes. Uncover and add potatoes, garbanzo beans, and salt. Add more boiling hot water if needed. Simmer on low heat for 15 minutes. Additional water may be added to reach soup consistency as needed. Add cilantro and black pepper; simmer for 5 minutes on low heat. Skim oil off the top, if desired. Serve over bread.

Shorwa-e-Gosphand

Chicken Soup ❖ *Yakhni-e-Murgh*

<u>40 minutes cooking time</u> (serves 4)
<u>Ingredients:</u>
2 medium yellow onions peeled and chopped
1 whole medium chicken cut into 16 pieces, skinless
3 roma tomatoes rough chopped
½ cup dry split yellow lentil soaked in water
3 cloves garlic minced
¼ cup fresh cilantro chopped
6 cups boiling hot water
4 tablespoons canola oil
1 teaspoon turmeric
2 teaspoons salt & black pepper to taste

In a large pot, sauté yellow onions in canola oil until translucent. Rinse and add chicken. Add turmeric, garlic, drained lentils and tomatoes. Add boiling hot water and cover pot, simmer on medium heat for 30 minutes. Additional water may be added to reach soup consistency as needed. Add cilantro and black pepper; simmer for 5 minutes on low heat. Serve hot.

Yakhni-e-Murgh

Chicken and Rice Soup ❖ *Shorwa Berenj*

<u>40 minutes cooking time</u> (serves 4)
<u>Ingredients:</u>
2 medium yellow onions peeled and chopped
2 lbs. chicken thigh cut into 1 inch pieces, skinless, boneless
1 cup tomato sauce
½ cup short-grain rice soaked in water
3 cloves garlic minced
¼ cup fresh cilantro chopped
6 cups boiling hot water
4 tablespoons canola oil
1 teaspoon turmeric
1 teaspoon ground coriander
2 teaspoons salt & black pepper to taste
Sour cream to garnish

In a large pot, sauté onions in canola oil until translucent. Rinse and add chicken. Sauté with garlic, until brown. Add turmeric, coriander, salt, and tomato sauce. Add boiling hot water and drained rice. Simmer on medium low heat and stir occasionally for 30 minutes. Add black pepper; simmer for 5 minutes on low heat. Serve hot with sour cream and cilantro on top.

SIMPLY AFGHAN

Shorwa Berenj

Beef and Bean Yogurt Soup ❖ *Mawshawa*

<u>1 hour cooking time</u> (serves 4)
<u>Ingredients:</u>
2 medium yellow onions 1 peeled and chopped, 1 minced finely
1 lb. ground beef
½ cup dry whole green lentil parboiled
½ cup canned garbanzo beans 15oz. drained
½ canned red kidney beans 15oz. drained
3 cloves garlic minced
1 cup Greek yogurt
5 cups boiling hot chicken broth
4 tablespoons canola oil
1 teaspoon turmeric
1 teaspoon ground coriander
2 teaspoons dried mint leaves *crushed*
4 teaspoons salt & black pepper to taste
Sour cream to garnish

    In a medium bowl, combine minced onion, ground beef, garlic, 2 teaspoons salt, black pepper and ground coriander.
    In a large pot, sauté remaining onions until brown. Add broth, lentils, garbanzo, red kidney beans, and turmeric. Shape the ground beef mixture into marble-sized balls and release them into the pot. Keep the pot at a simmer for 30 minutes. Take pot off heat and add the yogurt, remaining salt, and mint. Mix and serve immediately.

Mawshawa

Yellow Lentil Soup ❖ *Shorwa-e-Daal*

<u>50 minutes cooking time</u> (serves 4)
<u>Ingredients:</u>
2 medium yellow onions peeled and chopped
3 roma tomatoes rough chopped
1 cup yellow lentil soaked in water
3 cloves garlic minced
¼ cup fresh cilantro chopped
4 cups boiling hot water
¼ cup & 1 tablespoon canola oil
4 tablespoons whole wheat flour
1 teaspoon turmeric
¼ teaspoon ground cayenne pepper
1 teaspoon ground coriander
3 teaspoons salt & black pepper to taste

In a large pot, sauté onions in ¼ cup canola oil until translucent. Add turmeric, cayenne pepper, coriander, salt, flour and tomatoes. Cook until incorporated. Add boiling hot water and lentils. Simmer on medium low heat and stir occasionally for 30 minutes. Add black pepper; simmer for 10 minutes on low heat. In a separate small pan, fry garlic in remaining 1 tablespoon of oil until slightly brown. Turn off heat and pour garlic mixture on top of soup. Mix and serve.

Shorwa-e-Daal

2 RICE - BERENJ

An Afghan staple food, rice (*Berenj*) is almost always found on the dinner table. However, these *Berenj* recipes are full of flavor and each one boasts an interesting flavor profile. Disclaimer: rice can be very finicky, use your discretion and pay close attention to your rice pot.

> **I remember when…**
>
> It was the day of my son's graduation from high school and we decided to have the party at my house. My mother is 84 years old and has debilitating arthritis, especially in her hands. Her recipes for *Berenj* are famous in the family, *Qabuli Palau* in particular. That day, she led me step by step as to how the *Qabuli Palau* is prepared. It came out exactly how hers tastes and everyone thought she prepared it! Needless to say, it was a triumphant day for the whole family.
>
> *Qabuli Palau* recipe on page 17

White Rice ❖ *Chalow*

<u>30 minutes cooking time</u> (serves 4)
<u>Ingredients:</u>
2 cups long grain basmati rice
Salt to taste
¼ cup vegetable oil
3 cups boiling hot water
1 teaspoon ground cumin

Preheat oven to 350°F. Boil water in heavy medium-sized pot. Add salt, rice, oil, and cumin, cover pot and place in preheated oven for 20 minutes. Open lid, fluff up gently with a fork, replace lid and return to oven for an additional 10 minutes. Serve.

Chalow

Mixed Rice with Lamb ❖ *Dampokht-e-Gosphand*

<u>1 hour 20 minutes cooking time</u> (Serves 6)
<u>Ingredients:</u>
2 cups long grain basmati rice
Salt to taste
¼ cup vegetable oil
1 tablespoon Garam Masala
3 cups boiling hot water
2 medium yellow onions peeled and chopped
1 lb. lamb stew small cubed
3 roma tomatoes rough chopped

Preheat oven to 350°F. Brown onions in a heavy medium-sized pot with oil over medium heat. Add lamb and sauté until liquid is evaporated (about 30 minutes). Add tomatoes and cook until incorporated. Add salt, rice, Garam Masala, and water cover pot and place in oven for 20 minutes. Open lid, fluff up gently, replace lid and return to oven for an additional 20 minutes. Serve.

Dampokht-e-Gosphand

Uzbeki Style Afghan Rice ❖ *Qabuli Palau-e-Uzbeki*

<u>1 hour 50 minutes cooking time</u> (Serves 6)
<u>Ingredients:</u>
3 cups long grain basmati rice
Salt to taste
¼ cup vegetable oil
4 cups boiling hot water
1 teaspoon Garam Masala
2 lb. medium cut lamb shank
2 roma tomatoes chopped
2 medium yellow onions peeled and chopped
½ cup shredded lengthwise peeled carrots
¼ cup California raisins

Preheat oven to 350°F. In a heavy large-sized pot, soften onion over medium heat with vegetable oil. Add lamb, salt and brown. Add tomatoes and cook until incorporated. Add hot water to cover meat and cover pot with heat on simmering. Cook until tender, about 30 minutes.

In the same pot meat has cooked in, add rice, boiling hot water, Garam masala, carrots and raisins over top, cover pot. Place pot into the preheated oven and cook for 30 minutes. Open lid, fluff up gently, replace lid and return to oven for 20 minutes. Serve.

Qabuli Palau-e-Uzbeki

Mung Bean Rice ❖ *Mawsh Palau*

<u>1 hour 20 minutes cooking time</u> (Serves 6)
<u>Ingredients:</u>
2 cups long grain basmati rice
1 cup mung bean
Salt to taste
1 teaspoon Garam Masala
¼ cup vegetable oil
1 medium yellow onion peeled and chopped
3 roma tomatoes chopped
5 cups boiling hot water

Aside in a small pot, boil mung beans in 2 cups of water for 10 minutes. Preheat oven to 350°F.

In heavy medium-sized pot, brown onions with oil over medium heat. Add tomatoes and cook until incorporated. Add remaining 3 cups boiling hot water and drained beans from small pot, boil for 10 minutes. Add salt, rice, oil, and Garam Masala, cover pot. Transfer pot into preheated oven and cook for 30 minutes. Open lid, fluff up gently, and place back into the oven for an additional 20 minutes. Serve with *Qorma*.

Mawsh Palau

Lamb Soft Rice ❖ *Shola-e-Goshtee*

<u>1 hour 50 minutes cooking time</u> (Serves 6)
<u>Ingredients:</u>
2 cups short grain Calrose rice
1 cup green dried mung beans
Salt and black pepper to taste
2 tablespoons dried dill
½ teaspoon cayenne pepper
½ cup vegetable oil
6 cups boiling hot water
2 lb. small cut boneless lamb leg
3 roma tomatoes chopped
2 medium yellow onions peeled and chopped
1 cup canned garbanzo beans
1 cup canned red kidney beans

Aside, in separate bowls, soak rice and beans in water for one hour. Preheat oven to 350°F.

In a large heavy large-sized pot, soften onion over medium heat with oil. Add lamb and brown (about 20 minutes). Add tomatoes, pepper, cayenne, dill, salt and cook until incorporated. Add separate hot water to cover meat and cover pot with heat on simmering. Cook until tender, about 30 minutes.

Add drained rice and mung beans along with the boiling hot water. Place into oven and cook covered for 40 minutes. Add canned drained beans and additional water if needed, stir and continue to cook covered in oven for 20 minutes. Serve with pickles or afghan salad.

SIMPLY AFGHAN

Shola-e-Goshtee

3 STEWS - QORMA

Given the nomadic lifestyles of many Afghans, finding and storing fresh meat is unrealistic. Meats are usually cured, dried, then reconstituted in stews (*Qormas*) resulting in a delicious main course served with rice or bread.

I remember when…

In Afghanistan about 37 years ago we had some guests over from a nearby village at our home. My mom made *Qorma-e-Bamya* with lamb, *Berenj*, and an Afghan salad. She handed me fresh *naan* bread and *Qorma* to serve the guests. By the time I had returned to the kitchen to retrieve the *Berenj*, the guests had finished the *Qorma*! The guests quickly picked up on my mother's irritation and dirty looks because the *Berenj* was supposed to be eaten with the *Qorma*. "The *Qorma* was too good!" the guests exclaimed with guilt.

Qorma-e-Bamya recipe on page 26

Potato Stew ❖ *Qorma-e-Kachaloo*

40 minutes cooking time (Serves 4)
Ingredients:
1 medium yellow onions peeled and chopped
6 medium russet potatoes peeled and quartered
4 roma tomatoes chopped
¼ cup cilantro minced
4 cloves garlic
¼ cup vegetable oil
½ cup boiling hot water
Salt to taste
½ teaspoon black ground pepper
½ teaspoon turmeric

Brown onions with oil over medium low heat in a medium-sized pot. Add tomatoes and cook until incorporated. Add garlic, black pepper, salt, turmeric, and potatoes. Stir ingredients in pot. Add boiling hot water, lower heat to simmer, cover and cook for 20 minutes, stirring occasionally. Uncover and add cilantro. Serve with rice or bread.

Qorma-e-Kachaloo

Okra Stew ❖ *Qorma-e-Bamya*

<u>30 minutes cooking time </u>(Serves 4)
<u>Ingredients:</u>
2 lb. fresh or frozen okra tips and tops removed
6 roma tomatoes chopped
6 cloves garlic
¼ cup vegetable oil
Salt to taste
½ teaspoon black ground pepper
½ teaspoon turmeric

In a medium-sized pot, add oil and tomatoes, cook on medium low heat until incorporated. Add garlic, black pepper, salt, turmeric, and okra. Stir ingredients in pot gently using a wooden spoon once, lower heat to simmer, cover and cook for 20 minutes, stirring gently occasionally. Serve with rice or bread.

Qorma-e-Bamya

Cauliflower Stew ❖ *Qorma-e-Gulpi*

<u>30 minutes cooking time</u> (Serves 4)
<u>Ingredients:</u>
1 white cauliflower core removed and broken down to medium florets
6 roma tomatoes chopped
6 cloves garlic
¼ cup vegetable oil
Salt to taste
½ teaspoon black ground pepper
½ teaspoon turmeric

In a medium-sized pot, add oil and tomatoes, cook on medium low heat until incorporated. Add garlic, black pepper, salt, turmeric, and cauliflower. Stir ingredients in pot gently with a wooden spoon, lower heat to simmer, cover and cook for 20 minutes, stirring gently occasionally. Serve with rice or bread.

Qorma-e-Gulpi

Lentil Stew ❖ *Qorma-e-Daal*

40 minutes cooking time (Serves 4)
Ingredients:
1 medium yellow onions peeled and chopped
2 cups yellow lentil
4 roma tomatoes chopped
¼ cup cilantro minced
4 cloves garlic
¼ cup vegetable oil
1 cup boiling hot water
Salt to taste
½ teaspoon black ground pepper
½ teaspoon turmeric

Soak lentil in water separately in small bowl. Brown onions with oil over medium heat in a medium-sized pot. Add tomatoes and cook until incorporated. Add garlic, black pepper, salt, turmeric and lentils (drained). Stir ingredients in pot. Add boiling hot water, lower to medium low heat, cover and cook for 20 minutes, stirring occasionally. Uncover and add cilantro. Serve with rice or bread.

SIMPLY AFGHAN

Qorma-e-Daal

4   KABOBS

There are many variations of kabobs from the Mediterranean to the Far East. Afghan cuisine is not as plain as that of its neighbors to the west, however not as spicy as its neighbor's cuisine to the east. Afghani kabob is well seasoned, yet not disturbingly spicy.

I remember when…

I used to live on the same street as my mother. One day, I had invited some guests over to my house for dinner and out of respect to my mother, they stopped by her place. Customary to Afghan traditions, my mother invited them in when she was having a casual family dinner with my brothers and sister. My mother had made *Kabob-e-Seekhee-e-Murgh* along with other dishes. My guests were in such rapture over my mother's cooking that they filled up at her house. By the time they got to my home, the guests were too full to even touch my food!

Kabob-e-Seekhee-e-Murgh recipe on page 35

Ground Beef Kabob ❖ *Kabob-e-Seekhee-e-Kofta*

30 minutes cooking time (Serves 6)
Ingredients:
2 lbs. ground chuck (80/20 lean-to-fat ratio)
1 medium yellow onions peeled and finely blended in a food processor
¼ teaspoon of saffron strands steeped in 1 tablespoon of hot water
1 teaspoon salt
1 teaspoon black pepper

Place processed onion in a strainer to remove liquid, use pulp. Mix all the ingredients in a large bowl with a fork. Refrigerate for at least 2 hours, up to 24 hours. Form beef mixture around a metal skewer and refrigerate for 1 hour. Prepare barbeque, coal burning is best. Barbeque over medium high heat until beef is cooked to medium (10-15 minutes). Serve hot with rice or bread.

SIMPLY AFGHAN

Kabob-e-Seekhee-e-Kofta

Chicken Kabob ❖ *Kabob-e-Seekhee-Murgh*

<u>35 minutes cooking time</u> (Serves 6)
<u>Ingredients:</u>
2 lbs. chicken breast skinless boneless cut into one-inch cubes
2 teaspoons garlic finely minced
1 medium yellow onions minced finely in a food processor
1 teaspoon salt
1 teaspoon black pepper
1 teaspoon ground coriander
1 teaspoon ground black cardamom
1 teaspoon ground cumin
½ cup Greek yogurt
1 cup vegetable oil

Place processed onion in a strainer, use liquid only. Mix all the ingredients in a large bowl. Refrigerate for at least 2 hours, up to 24 hours. Skewer chicken on metal skewers. Prepare barbeque, coal burning is best. Barbeque over medium high heat until chicken is cooked (10-15 minutes). Serve hot with rice or bread.

SIMPLY AFGHAN

Kabob-e-Seekhee-e-Murgh

Beef Kabob ❖ *Kabob-e-Seekhee-e-Gow*

<u>35 minutes cooking time </u>(Serves 6)
<u>Ingredients:</u>
2 lbs. filet mignon cleaned and cut into one-inch cubes
2 teaspoons garlic finely minced
1 medium yellow onions minced finely in a food processor
1 teaspoon salt
1 teaspoon black pepper
½ cup Greek yogurt
1 cup vegetable oil

Place processed onion in a strainer, use liquid only. Mix all the ingredients in a large bowl. Refrigerate for at least 2 hours, up to 24 hours. Skewer beef on metal skewers. Prepare barbeque, coal burning is best. Barbeque over medium high heat until beef is cooked (8-10 minutes). Serve hot with rice or bread.

Kabob-e-Seekhee-e-Gow

Lamb Kabob ❖ *Kabob-e-Seekhee-e-Gosphand*

35 minutes cooking time (Serves 6)
Ingredients:
2 lbs. lamb leg boneless cut into one-inch cubes
2 teaspoons garlic finely minced
1 medium yellow onions minced finely in a food processor
1 teaspoon salt
1 teaspoon black pepper
½ cup Greek yogurt
1 cup vegetable oil

Place processed onion in a strainer, use liquid only. Mix all the ingredients in a large bowl. Refrigerate for at least 2 hours, up to 24 hours. Skewer lamb on metal skewers. Prepare barbeque, coal burning is best. Barbeque over medium high heat until lamb is cooked to medium (9-11 minutes). Serve hot with rice or bread.

SIMPLY AFGHAN

Kabob-e-Seekhee-e-Gosphand

ABOUT THE AUTHOR

An Afghan refugee of war in the early 1980's, Kochai Farhad made Southern California home. Having never dismissed her cultural roots, Kochai has kept traditions alive by cooking authentic Afghan food often and with passion. After a nearly 4 year tour in Afghanistan recently, working with the U.S. army as a linguist, Kochai's passion for her cooking was only heightened. While deployed, she would use what little ingredients she could find on base to create dishes for her fellow coworkers. Now back with a renewed hope, Kochai is ready to share her recipes, stories, and know how with American home cooks.

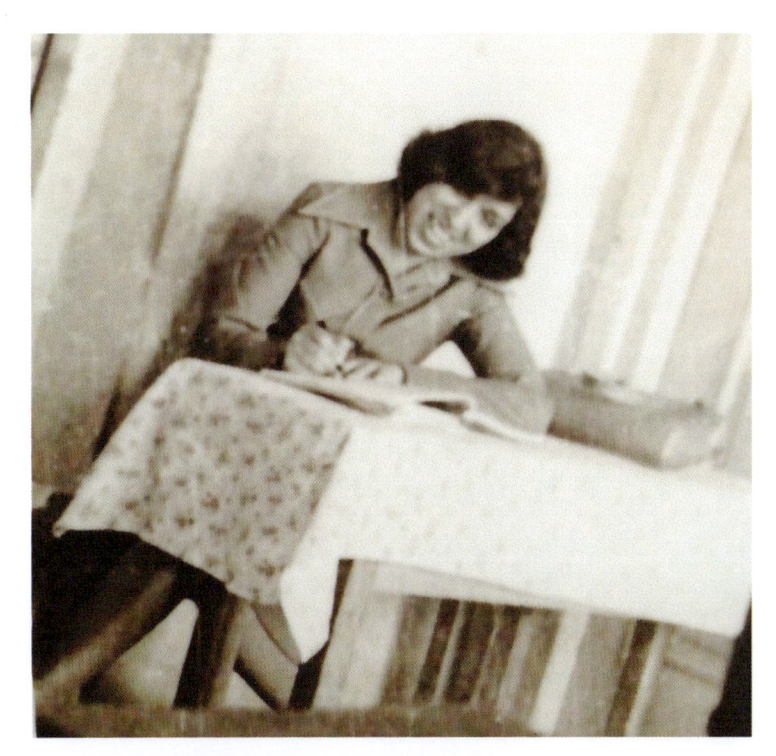

1974 Teaching in Kabul

1993 with Joseph

Printed in Great Britain
by Amazon